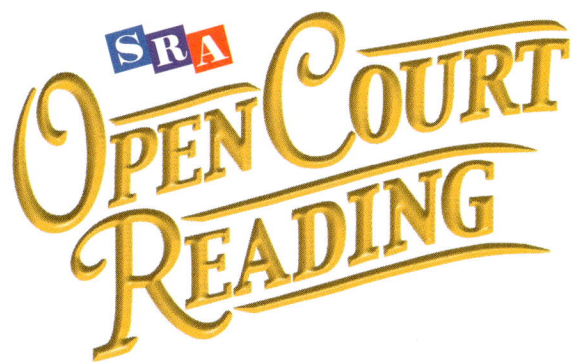

Wendell's Pets

A Division of The McGraw·Hill Companies

Columbus, Ohio

www.sra4kids.com

SRA/McGraw-Hill

A Division of The McGraw·Hill Companies

Copyright © 2002 by SRA/McGraw-Hill.

All rights reserved. Except as permitted under the United States Copyright Act, no part of this publication may be reproduced or distributed in any form or by any means, or stored in a database or retrieval system, without prior written permission from the publisher.

Printed in the United States of America.

Send all inquiries to:
SRA/McGraw-Hill
8787 Orion Place
Columbus, OH 43240-4027

ISBN 0-07-569477-8

3 4 5 6 7 8 9 DBH 05 04 03 02

Wendell's Pets

Wendell had lots of pets.
Wendell had his cat and his duck.

Wendell had his rabbit and his lizard.
Wendell had frogs and a tub for his bugs.

Wendell's pets went to his class,
and his class was glad.
But Mr. Webb was not glad.

Wendell's pets hopped, scratched, and wiggled. "Wendell, you will have to put your pets away," said Mr. Webb.

"Here!" said Wendell.
"With me!"
And Wendell's pets sat with him!